How to s

ASSESSMENT CENTRES

TROTMAN

This first edition published in 1995
by Trotman and Company Ltd
12 Hill Rise, Richmond, Surrey TW10 6UA

© Trotman and Company Limited 1995

British Library Cataloguing in Publication Data
A catalogue record for this book is available from the
British Library.

ISBN 0 85660 349 X

Printed and bound in Great Britain

ABOUT THE AUTHOR

Mary Wilson graduated with a BA from the University of Capetown. She now works as Assistant Secretary at the Association of Graduate Recruiters. She has worked in numerous organisations - ranging from gold mines to the University of Cambridge and as an industrial and financial journalist.

CONTENTS

WHAT HAPPENS AT AN ASSESSMENT CENTRE?

WHAT IS AN ASSESSMENT CENTRE?

An assessment centre isn't really a place – it's an event set up by an organisation that's looking to recruit graduates. During this event, a whole series of exercises and tests are 'centralised' for the assessors to apply them to candidates quickly and efficiently. So there are three components to an assessment centre – **you** (the candidate), the **exercises** and the **assessors**.

Some organisations, like the armed forces, have purpose- built premises where they select people throughout the year but most companies usually get a group of applicants together at a convenient venue, like a hotel or conference centre.

WHEN WILL I ENCOUNTER ONE?

Most often after your first interview with the organisation or after some sort of pre-selection. If they like the sound of you from your application form or from the milkround, they'll invite you to attend an assessment centre to take a closer look at you.

HOW LONG DOES AN ASSESSMENT CENTRE LAST?

Usually between one and two days, although if you've been invited by the armed forces or the police, it could last longer because they will put you through more exercises and physical tasks like obstacle courses. Or else they may have additional tests, like the RAF tests for spatial reasoning, reflexes etc.

HOW OFTEN ARE THEY HELD?

It varies with the size of the organisation and how many graduates they recruit – from twice a year to twice a week.

WHAT SORT OF ORGANISATIONS USE ASSESSMENT CENTRES TO SELECT PEOPLE?

Because they're so expensive to run, it's mostly the larger ones and those which offer higher starting salaries. But the use of these centres is increasing – 60 per cent of member organisations surveyed by the Association of Graduate Recruiters now use them.

WILL ALL THE OTHER CANDIDATES BE UNIVERSITY STUDENTS OR GRADUATES?

Not necessarily. Some centres are for all, including those with lower educational qualifications or varying age groups.

All assessment centres should reflect what the actual working situation with that firm is like and the assessment centre will be made up of the same types of candidates. Some organisations concentrate on recruiting mainly graduates for management. At others the management training programme is open to anyone who shows potential. It all depends of the type of job you've applied for and the type of organisation.

HOW MANY CANDIDATES WILL THERE BE THERE?

This can vary. Some assessment centres, if they have the premises and the assessors, are able to 'process' a lot of people at the same time; others can only do a few in consecutive events. Whatever happens, you'll be in a group that's small enough to allow the assessors to observe your behaviour very closely but large enough to allow interaction between members of the group – about 10 people per group.

WILL THE CANDIDATES BE DIVIDED BY SEX?

Absolutely not! What the exercises try to simulate is everyday situations in the working life of an organisation. So, unless you've applied to a convent or a monastery, it's everyone in together.

Some assessment centres may have a preponderance of one sex or another but that only reflects the applications the firms have had. Some careers attract more of one sex than another – for example, the armed forces tend to attract more men while retailing attracts more women.

WHY DO ORGANISATIONS USE THEM?

Research has shown that the assessment centre is the most effective method for predicting successful performance in the job that candidates are applying for.

WHAT HAPPENS AT AN ASSESSMENT CENTRE?

It's a very intense and concentrated event – more for the assessors than for the candidates, so you'll probably be unaware of most of what's going on in the background! This book will explain in detail a lot of things that happen.

All centres aim to obtain information about your current or potential competence through a sophisticated series of appropriate selection techniques. The assessment centre event provides an opportunity to observe your behaviour directly. The organisers arrange a number of exercises, for example, group discussions, each of which allows them to look at a different aspect of your behaviour.

The information obtained is measured against a series of characteristics that are relevant to the job.

IT TOOK ME HOURS TO FILL IN COMPANY X's APPLICATION FORM. WHAT MORE DO THEY WANT TO KNOW ABOUT ME?

They want to know how you behave in certain circumstances, as opposed to obtaining information from your application form, references and your academic record.

WHAT HAS MY BEHAVIOUR GOT TO DO WITH IT?

The way anyone behaves is an indication of the characteristics they have. The assessment centre will look at aspects of your behaviour but in relation only to the characteristics that are necessary for successful performance in a particular job with a particular organisation – they certainly won't be looking at your inner soul!

They're also not expecting you to perform as if you've already had five years of management experience. What the selection procedures are designed to find is your potential.

4

YOU MEAN, THEY'RE LOOKING FOR ALL MY WEAK POINTS?

Not at all. Although assessment centres are very stringent in their requirements, they're very positive in their approach. What they're looking for is for evidence of good qualities and to what degree you demonstrate them.

HOW DOES AN ASSESSMENT CENTRE RELATE TO THE JOB I'VE APPLIED FOR?

The firm's job advert, its application form and its brochure should all be giving out the same indication of what sorts of skills the firm is looking for. A well thought-out graduate recruitment campaign will have a certain unity about the message the firm is trying to convey. If you've done your research, you yourself will have decided which organisations you'd rather work for.

But organisations are starting to contract outside consultants to find graduates for them. This means that you could be invited to an assessment centre and not know what job in which organisation it is for! This may be a bit disorientating but this book will give you an idea of the general sorts of skills that recruiters are looking for in graduates.

The assessment centre allows the organisation to look at whether you've got the right mix of these skills for them. From their knowledge of your university course and from your application form, they know that you'll satisfy the academic needs of the job, although if it's a technical position you've applied for, you may also be interviewed by a technical manager. It's your skills that they'll be interested in, and the best way to find if you have them is to get you to demonstrate them at an assessment centre.

5

WHO DECIDES WHAT SORT OF CHARACTERISTICS ARE NECESSARY FOR A PARTICULAR JOB AND HOW DO THEY GO ABOUT IT?

It's the occupational psychologists or personnel specialists who research an existing job in great detail – the content of the job, the people who've been successful in it. They analyse the job in terms of:

- What objectives are to be met by the job?
- What tasks does the individual have to perform to meet these objectives?
- What skills and capabilities do individuals need to perform these tasks?
- What additional skills do individuals require to handle the context in which the job is carried out?

As well as the specific job, all sorts of other things are also taken into consideration – the organisation itself and its management structure, the corporate culture, the external environment.

The specialists then draw up a 'job specification'. From this they can describe a 'profile' of the job and the key capabilities or 'criteria' that are needed for effective performance of that job. These criteria can range from relatively easy things to assess like the standard of numeracy or level of foreign language required to more difficult concepts like 'leadership'.

If they want to survive, companies have to recognise that they have to live with change in the modern world. This means that sometimes the specialists have to analyse jobs or job roles that don't even exist yet. Because graduates are a future resource, an organisation may be recruiting you not for what you'll be able to do in six months' time but for five or ten years hence. So the job role in the future may need the 'ability to handle change' as an example of a criterion.

6

Equally, because you're a future resource, the firm's management development programme is another factor to be taken into account.

WHAT EXACTLY ARE THE COMPETENCIES THAT ORGANISATIONS ARE LOOKING FOR IN CANDIDATES?

Different firms will have their own set of competencies which they require candidates to demonstrate at assessment centres. Few will reveal exactly what they expect from candidates but this is general list:

- **Intellectual**
  Strategic perspective
  Analysis and Judgement
  Planning and Organising
- **Interpersonal**
  Managing others
  Persuasiveness
  Assertiveness
  Oral and verbal communication
- **Adaptability**
  Versatility
  Resilience
- **Results Orientation**
  Energy and Initiative
  Achievement motivation.

WHAT IS THE NEXT STAGE TOWARDS AN ASSESSMENT CENTRE?

The specialists then set out typical 'behavioural indicators' for each of these criteria. For example, they will give concrete examples of behaviour to illustrate the criterion of 'leadership' with particular reference to the organisation you've applied to.

Or else for the criterion 'ability to think on his/her feet', they might illustrate an example of being able to cope with the unexpected, like suddenly being asked to do some quick mental calculations in the middle of a totally different situation without the benefit of a calculator!

THIS ALL SEEMS RATHER VAGUE AND WOOLLY!

From the behavioural indicators and the job situation analysis, the specialists are able to devise a series of exercises which elicit evidence of a certain type of behaviour pattern. For example, a group discussion will show to what extent each participant demonstrates evidence of leadership skills, ability to negotiate, ability to present an argument, among other capabilities.

GIVE ME AN EXAMPLE OF A BEHAVIOURAL INDICATOR

Initially a skill is likely to be expressed in the abstract – eg 'communication'. This can then be interpreted into a more concrete example of performance: 'Presents clearly both orally and in writing. Displays listening skills and an awareness of the impact of personal appearance and non-verbal communication.'

Another example – 'flexibility'. One organisation defines this as: 'The ability to respond promptly and effectively to changes or unexpected developments; the ability to respond with different arguments, methods or leadership styles in order to reach a goal; the ability to modify behaviour and style yet remain effective.'

In more detail, the organisation assesses whether '. . . the candidate shows a variety of approaches and influencing styles in order to achieve a goal without having to change his/her mind? Is he or she prepared to deviate from the original plan to gain advantage or facilitate discussion? Or does he or she, at the slightest opposition, change the decision for no good reason? A change of mind is only acceptable if it is in response to changing information, changing circumstances or reasoned argument, not because it is the easiest option.

Can the candidate cope with unfamiliar material and with uncertainty? Can he/she balance conflicting objectives? Or progress several issues concurrently? Can he/she modify their own arguments to reflect the approaches or views of others so that the group can attain its goal? Can he/she alter their approach to others to gain their agreement or commitment?

Negative indicators: fails to grasp problems; resists ideas and changes of direction and fails to integrate them into own stance; perseveres with stale ideas; keeps returning to the same issues.'

BUT I'M ON TRACK TO GET A FIRST OR A TOP 2.1! SURELY THAT'S ENOUGH TO SATISFY ANY EMPLOYER?

No, it isn't. Organisations now realise that, for most jobs, academic achievement alone is unlikely to lead to success. With the rising supply of graduates, employers are increasingly using what they broadly call 'personal transferable skills' as a way of selecting recruits. It is these skills that appear in one way or another in the criteria for assessment.

SURELY EMPLOYERS ARE ALL LOOKING FOR THE SAME TYPE OF SKILLS?

Not really. Employers differ enormously. Each organisation, even departments within an organisation, interprets personal transferable skills in a way to suit particular job roles.

Because employers are looking for different things in their recruits, they give these qualities different weightings. For example, a heavy engineering company will look for very different skills mix from an advertising agency; or a City merchant bank and a firm of lawyers will have diverging skill requirements.

SHOW ME SOME EXAMPLES OF HOW A CERTAIN CRITERION CAN BE INTERPRETED INTO DIFFERENT SKILLS

Take 'leadership' for example:

- One organisation might interpret it as: 'Communication, ability to influence people, managing situations, and self-confidence'
- But another employer might define the components slightly differently: 'An analytical mind, self-motivation, capacity for solving practical problems, the ability to motivate and inspire others'.
- Yet another recruiter may look at it from another angle: 'Leadership is the ability to guide or direct individuals (subordinates, peers, superiors) or a group towards task accomplishment without necessarily relying on authority and position.'

So you can see that the leadership qualities that organisations look for have nothing to do with arrogance and aggression.

I'M STILL NOT CLEAR EXACTLY HOW THESE CRITERIA AND THE SKILLS EMPLOYERS WANT RELATE TO THE ASSESSMENT CENTRE

All the tests and exercises you do at an assessment centre are designed not only to generate evidence of the skills required but also reflect the tasks and activities of the target job. So you will find that the exercises especially are like 'real life' situations you would encounter in the job you've applied for – situations where you would need to use the skills the employer is looking for.

If, for example, you've applied for a job in retail, the exercises might simulate the sort of daily problems a store manager would encounter and the assessors watch how you deal with them.

Sometimes this may come as a bit of a shock to a candidate and they make up their mind there and then that applying to Company X was a *big* mistake! Assessment centres are often as much about applicants selecting an employer as vice versa. If this happens to you, carry on with the assessment centre and do your best because if you treat it casually or drop out, you can make things difficult for the other participants. You never know – you may be offered a job, which you can always turn down. Anyway, going through an assessment centre is an excellent learning experience and prepares you for the one with the organisation you *really* want to work for.

OK, SO I'VE GOT THE GENERAL CONCEPT BEHIND AN ASSESSMENT CENTRE. WHAT'S THE FIRST THING I CAN EXPECT?

You'll probably be sent instructions about how and when to get to the place where the assessment centre is being held. You may be asked to arrive the night before it starts so that you can meet the other applicants and settle in. The organisers will try their best to make you feel comfortable and at ease because they really do want you to do your best.

A CLASSMATE OF MINE DID PSYCHOMETRIC AND OTHER WRITTEN TESTS BEFORE SHE WENT TO THE ASSESSMENT CENTRE. WHY HAVEN'T I BEEN ASKED TO DO THEM?

Organisations differ as to when they administer these tests. Some firms do them earlier in the selection process – for sandwich or placement students, for example. Others prefer to do them at the milkround interview.

At an assessment centre, they're usually held early on so that they can be analysed while other exercises are taking place.

WHAT IF I FAIL THESE TESTS RIGHT AT THE BEGINNING OF THE ASSESSMENT CENTRE?

Only at a few places, like the RAF for obvious reasons, do test results play a crucial part in selection – fighter pilots can't have poor eye-to-hand co-ordination! Some software companies, as another example, need high computer aptitude.

Elsewhere the results are usually only used to give an added dimension to the information from application forms and that which the assessors gather through direct contact with the candidates.

No single test or exercise can reveal someone's qualities – therefore the assessment centre approach is to combine a range of methods. Different tasks elicit evidence of certain skills and capabilities to different degrees. Assessors observe each person's behaviour in several different situations against the framework of the criteria that have been identified in the job analysis.

Therefore, if you feel you did badly on one test, remind yourself that it's only one of a series and it's not a question of passing or failing on a single exercise. The assessors certainly aren't making any decisions at this early stage. Also remind yourself that every person in your group is going to do not so well in some exercises and better in others.

At some assessment centres, only the chairperson (see p. 23) is aware of the results of psychometric tests so as not to bias the assessors.

WHAT EXACTLY ARE THESE TESTS?

There are two main types: aptitude tests and personality questionnaires. **Aptitude tests** vary according to the aptitude requirements of the job. Most test numerical and verbal reasoning. Numeracy tests do not normally look for algebra or geometry – they usually involve analysis of tables of figures (eg sales reports) and graphs using basic arithmetic (percentages, proportions and ratios). Often the ace mathematician has forgotten all this and shows very little practical or commercial sense! And here's a tip – most of the time, you won't be allowed to use a calculator. **Verbal reasoning tests** often concentrate on the exact meaning of words and involve making logical deductions from paragraphs of information. Some recruiters add logical or diagrammatic reasoning questions. The majority of people don't finish the written tests as they usually include more questions than you can be expected to complete in the time allotted.

Personality questionnaires vary as much as organisations and jobs do. There are no right or wrong answers. They ask how you would behave in different situations, especially in relation to other people. They paint a picture of an individual and it is up to a skilled assessor, often an occupational psychologist, to judge how a person with that personality will perform on the job. These tests are useful in elucidating areas where it is difficult to observe behaviour directly – for example, thinking styles and emotional behaviour. They don't measure ability – they merely indicate a preferred pattern of behaviour – and they relate entirely to the job itself.

ARE ALL ASSESSMENT CENTRES THE SAME?

No, not at all – organisations and jobs differ. Because job content determines the exercises used, it follows that assessment centre programmes will vary as well, even by department within organisations. The skills required in a production engineer's job will be weighted differently from those in a legal department, for example. Although both departments may be looking for decision-making ability, for instance, it's interpreted differently by each.

However, the principles of all assessment centres are the same – namely, to elicit behavioural evidence from a candidate which can be judged against agreed criteria that are specific to the position advertised.

WHAT'S THE MOST COMMON TYPE OF EXERCISE?

In general, any activity that involves working with a group rather than on your own. With more and more emphasis being placed on working in teams in management today, assessors seek evidence of appropriate skills through a variety of group exercises. Most of these exercises simulate the sorts of daily group activities in the recruiting organisation. Group exercises are often scheduled early on as they help participants to settle in. Usually there will be six to ten people in a team, with one assessor to every two candidates. However, if a particular job does mainly involve one-to-one client meetings, then exercises which simulate these situations are important.

WHAT HAPPENS IN THE GROUP ACTIVITIES?

Group exercises can take the form of discussions of a general nature or focused on a particular problem which needs a group solution. You, or another member of the team, may have to give a presentation on the solution afterwards.

In group exercises, assessors look for behavioural evidence of your:

- participation and contribution
- analysis, presentation of a reasoned argument
- communication
- listening abilities
- negotiation and co-operation.

WHAT SORT OF THINGS CAN I EXPECT IN A GROUP DISCUSSION?

Discussion groups can be 'open' where participants discuss topics of a general nature introduced by the assessor. Or they can be more structured where group members discuss, draw up strategies and reach an agreed plan on a particular work-related problem from the information given to them. This could be a simulation or case study or a technical problem for science and engineering applicants.

In some discussion groups, each member is questioned about his or her solution by the team assessors. To allow assessment of written communication, they may also have to write an essay on it.

Discussion groups can take different forms:

- the 'leaderless' ones, where everyone has the same brief and goes into a meeting with an objective of achieving some sort of consensus decision;

- the 'assigned role' ones, where each person has a different brief so they go into the meeting with a hidden agenda. (This often results in conflict and participants are assessed on how well they handle it.)

In all discussion, the assessors judge how often you speak and the quality of your contributions – whether you're the leader or not. Bear in mind that the emphasis is on negotiation and consensus decision-making.

WHAT HAPPENS DURING PHYSICAL ACTIVITIES?

Group exercises can also take the form of physical tasks across obstacle courses. These can be 'leaderless' or 'own command' situations where everyone gets a turn to be the leader.

As the armed services operate in a pressurised environment, their testing reflect similar pressure and urgency. Testing for stress tolerance in civilian organisations, which operate in less extreme situations, is less demanding, although group exercises are always timed. Many civilian organisation put candidates under pressure to think quickly and accurately. Testing for stress tolerance may simply be a question of the person's ability to handle the assessment centre.

I'M ONLY 5 FT 2 IN. AND MY HOBBY IS PAINTING FLOWERS! SURELY THE 'RADIANT BEAUTY' COMPANY ISN'T GOING TO ASK ME TO COMPLETE AN OBSTACLE COURSE?

Some organisations do use physical tasks over obstacle courses, either inside or out of doors. But the object is not to find out

16

how physically fit you are – rather, to put you into an unfamiliar situation to see how you cope.

In team exercises, the most important thing is that these tasks need the co-operation of the whole group. They don't involve any tricks and are accomplished by co-ordinated physical effort.

Most of the time the obstacles in your way do not demand physical strength but ingenuity, good planning and teamwork. So in the assessors' eyes, you may perform better than the 18-stone Captain of Rugby who relies on his (or her!) physical fitness but is stumped when it comes to finding a way around a complex problem.

WHAT IS A CANDIDATE EXPECTED TO DO IN A PROBLEM-SOLVING PROJECT?

The person is often given a complex logistics or technical problem to resolve. In the armed forces this usually involves transporting equipment and people, over difficult terrain, in adverse conditions (eg bad weather, darkness) and with limited resources. Pressure is created by the fact that the situation is an emergency. Each person may be asked to write out his or her solution and then to justify the plan in a presentation, sometimes in an atmosphere of tension, with the audience asking questions or criticising the plan's faults in a way that may require instant modification or an alternative solution.

In all problem-solving projects, candidates are given a number of facts which they must select and prioritise. In civilian assessment centres, projects (often known as 'business games') are usually work related – interpreting tables, graphs, sales figures, for example. You may also be asked to give a presentation on the project.

17

WHAT ARE ASSESSORS LOOKING FOR IN THE PROBLEM-SOLVING PROJECTS?

These are some of the things:

- comprehension and clarity of thought
- ability to analyse and to make deductions
- ability to prioritise, plan and think the consequences through
- ability to take options through to conclusion
- determination
- confidence in own judgement
- creativity and imagination
- written and oral communication
- presentation skills
- mental agility
- reaction to pressure.

ARE INTERVIEWS AT ASSESSMENT CENTRES ANY DIFFERENT FROM NORMAL ONES?

As you would expect, the interview is one of the most widely used selection techniques, both as part of an assessment centre and on its own. Effective interviews are structured interviews, ie interviews that are based on criteria, and so these are the ones used at assessment centres, based on the same techniques. They are systematic, conducted by well trained interviewers and arranged in such a way that everything relates to the standard or criteria.

The atmosphere is generally relaxed and the interviewers will try to put you at your ease – although it's by no means a cosy chat! The questions are largely based on what you have written down in your application form. You'll probably be asked about your interests, achievements and ambitions and you'll have an opportunity to ask questions about the organisation and the job.

Interviewers really want to know what you're good at, what your strengths are and whether you're aware of your weaknesses and prepared to do anything about them.

I'VE HEARD MIXED REPORTS ABOUT INTERVIEWS. SURELY THEY'RE VERY SUBJECTIVE?

You're right in that there's quite a lot of controversy about them. Some recruiters regard them as a poor selection tool, only to be used with other tests – in fact, some large recruiters of graduates don't use them at all. They agree that they can be subjective and that they elicit information, not behavioural evidence.

At an assessment centre, the interview is used to gather additional evidence against certain skills and to explore others in greater depth, like motivation to do the job or technical knowledge. So you can expect to encounter technical specialists or line managers trained in interviewing. This can be a good opportunity to raise any questions you may have.

Bear in mind that organising and running an assessment centre is extremely expensive. Therefore no employer is going to waste time and money on a selection technique that is neither reliable (ie works in the same way every time) or valid (able to predict job success). Some organisations will schedule several structured interviews with different assessors or have two interviewers conducting the interview to ensure objectivity.

WHAT OTHER TYPES OF EXERCISES ARE THERE?

In-tray exercises   You're asked to deal with a representative sample of a day's post and other documents.

Again, they're looking for the ability to prioritise and make the right decisions relevant to the everyday problems in the working environment.

Role play   In this type of exercise, you're put into a devised situation and the assessors see what you would do in it – for example, how you would deal with an employee who is always late, or how you would negotiate a budget. The individual who is playing the part of the person you're interacting with represents a colleague in the organisation. He or she is thoroughly trained in the role but is not an assessor – someone else will be observing and recording your behaviour.

Fact-finding exercises   This is similar to a role play with the aim of the exercise being for the candidate to extract relevant information form the resource person. The candidate then has to reach a decision.

AM I GOING TO BE JUDGED ON MY ACCENT OR MY TABLE MANNERS?

No successful organisation is ever going to do that. It would be totally counterproductive to their interests – if they did, they'd miss some very good candidates. These sorts of things have nothing to do with your ability to perform well in the job – you are being judged entirely on your own merits. Remember that you are never under observation during social events, meals and coffee breaks.

I NEED CONVINCING THAT THERE WON'T BE ANY RACIAL DISCRIMINATION. HOW DO ASSESSMENT CENTRES MAKE SURE THAT THE JUDGEMENT OF THEIR ASSESSORS IS OBJECTIVE?

All employers are legally required to show that their selection processes are fair. Like sex and marital status, discrimination on the grounds of race, colour, nationality or ethnic or national origins is covered by legislation. Assessment centres reduce subjective judgement to a minimum.

The use of criteria-based techniques means that the same standards are applied to all candidates. You're being compared against an ideal standard, ie the criteria for the job that the psychologists identified well before the assessment centre takes place. This means that you're *not* being compared with other people on the assessment centre and that the same standard will be applied to candidates at an assessment centre in six months time.

Remember, it's not only unfair to candidates to apply standards that vary but it's also a waste of time and money for the organisation to do so.

I'M A MATURE STUDENT. WILL THAT MAKE ANY DIFFERENCE?

It shouldn't, unless the training requirements of the job mean that they have to set an age limit – for example, in the armed forces. In fact, you may have the advantage. Your maturity and greater experience could help when it comes to working in a team or in decision-making. Just make sure you demonstrate your flexibility!

HOW DO ASSESSORS ACHIEVE OBJECTIVITY?

First of all, they're very well trained. Secondly, objectivity is ensured through the consistency of the procedures and consistency of judgement. There are three stages to objective assessment:
Observe and Record examples of behaviour
Classify examples according to profile criteria
Evaluate performance on each criterion on a rating scale.

WHAT HAPPENS DURING THE FIRST STAGE – OBSERVING AND RECORDING?

The assessors who are observing your performance during the exercises start by recording *very accurately* what you say and do. This forms the raw material.

They make no judgements at this stage. If, for example, an assessor hears someone say, 'Why don't we prepare an agenda?' but records 'Good at planning and organising', this would not be allowed because the assessor is classifying and evaluating behaviour too early on.

AND IN CLASSIFYING BEHAVIOURAL EXAMPLES?

They then classify the recorded evidence, both positive and negative, into the appropriate criteria (eg leadership, communication, flexibility) and write it up against each criterion. Each example of behaviour is kept distinct.

HOW DO THEY EVALUATE THE CANDIDATE'S PERFORMANCE?

The next stage is to select from the recorded evidence the most significant examples of a particular criterion or skill. These are evaluated qualitatively against the standard required on the job and given a numerical rating.

The assessors consider the behavioural examples of a particular criterion together. However, they rate each criterion independently because some people may score highly on one skill and low on another. For example, a candidate with a '6' in flexibility can score a '1' on decision making.

The assessors do not 'average out' positive and negative examples of behaviour.

I STILL NEED TO BE CONVINCED ABOUT THE ASSESSORS' OBJECTIVE JUDGEMENT. HOW CAN I BE SURE THAT THEY'RE NOT BIASED?

The aim at an assessment centre is that each candidate must be given an equal chance, whatever his or her background, whoever the other candidates are and whoever the assessors are. This is achieved by strict adherence to the standard and to the procedures. While subjectivity and bias cannot be entirely eliminated, other procedures should be in place to keep it to a minimum – as we have mentioned, often only the chair of the assessment centre has all the facts about a candidate lest knowledge of an aptitude test or a headmaster's report, for example, colour the judgement of other assessors.

For the same reason, assessors never discuss people's performances between themselves until the final evaluation conference.

Some procedures are very strict indeed. At some assessment centres, to ensure the same starting point for everyone before the physical tasks, assessors have to brief each group of candidates from a standard script. At some structured interviews, the assessors read out exactly the same questions to each candidate.

AS WELL AS THE PROCEDURES, HOW ELSE DO THEY TRY TO ENSURE OBJECTIVITY?

One of the most important means of eliminating subjectivity is the use of trained assessors. Training ensures accuracy, consistency and hence objectivity. To give the fullest dimension to an assessment centre, some assessors are trained to look for different qualities from different angles.

WHO ARE THE ASSESSORS?

In civilian organisations, these assessors are often drawn from line management, especially in technical areas. Quite often both a personnel professional and a trained line manager will observe each candidate. The armed forces have full-time assessors who have been officers in the various branches of the services.

HOW ARE THE ASSESSORS TRAINED?

They have to learn the skills of observing, recording, classifying and evaluating, and to carry out these skills as separate exercises in order to be objective.

WHAT ARE THEY TRAINED TO OBSERVE AND RECORD?

They watch participants at an assessment centre across a range of exercises. They learn to scrutinise both verbal and non-verbal behaviour and to record accurately while they are observing.

Their instructors make them aware of common faults – such as prejudice, lack of concentration or reference to stereotypes. They are also trained to recognise any tendencies to generalise good performance from one criterion to another. Or to expect subconsciously that, because a person has performed badly in one exercise, they will do the same in the next. So don't think that if you did badly in one exercise, it will affect the assessors' opinion of how you do in the following ones.

Assessors also learn not to allow first impressions to colour conflicting information observed later. Don't ever think, 'That assessor took an instant dislike to me' – a trained assessor will never do so.

FOR HOW LONG ARE ASSESSORS TRAINED?

It varies from organisation to organisation, from a few days, with refresher courses, to several weeks. If an assessor is not up to scratch, they're not used.

WHO ASSESSES THE ASSESSORS?

Occupational psychologists and experienced and successful assessors. You may also notice during the assessment centre that there is one person who does not appear to be observing and recording but who discreetly appears and disappears during the exercises. This is the chair of the assessment centre. His or her job is to manage the process and to maintain quality control. They may check every report and go back to the assessor to clarify their understanding or to ask for changes. The chair monitors assessors' abilities to perform their role. Some chairs also act as assessors. Furthermore, assessors' reports and evaluations are statistically monitored to pick up any discrepancies.

WHAT DOES THE CHAIR CHECK?

He or she has to make certain that all the procedures that ensure that an assessment centre is as objective as possible are being complied with. The chair's job is cut out checking all aspects of these procedures as they are happening and later, the assessors' notes.

The chair's checklist is too lengthy to detail here but these are some of the things he or she would look at:

- that during the Observation and Recording stage, the assessor has collected enough evidence against all the criteria;
- that the data is not judgemental or interpretative and that it's correctly classified;
- that there's a balance of positive and negative data;
- the reason for a 'zero' evaluation, for example;
- that the assessor's standard of evaluation is in line with the others.

THIS WHOLE ASSESSMENT CENTRE SYSTEM SEEMS TO BE VERY COMPLEX

Yes, it is – and very concentrated. What this book has described so far is to some extent an ideal assessment centre and whether this is ever achievable is open to question.

Most centres contain, to a greater or lesser extent, many of the elements we've described. As with most business operations, thoroughness has to be balanced against cost.

By now you will be aware that it is a very expensive process – the initial design by specialists; taking well paid managers off their jobs for training and the actual event; premises, accommodation, travel etc.

Selection marks the beginning of a considerable investment and the cost of graduate training, plus the costs just mentioned, could amount to well over £15,000 – or even £3 million for a fighter pilot!

To make sure that it is worth all the time and money, organisations have to be certain that it is effective. This means that the process *must*, as far as possible, select the right people

26

for the organisation. Employees' performance during management training and in the job will then be monitored carefully. The assessment centre process itself needs to be constantly reassessed and all this adds to the cost.

WHY DO ORGANISATIONS GO TO ALL THIS TROUBLE?

There is very little slack in the modern firm. Because there are now fewer managers and these hold higher responsibility earlier on in their careers, it is important to select the right ones.

WHY NOT JUST PICK SOME GRADUATES, PUT THEM ON THE JOB, SEE HOW THEY PERFORM AND FIRE THEM IF THEY'RE NO GOOD?

Because that's even more expensive and bad for the firm! Staff are the firm's most important and costly resource. Organisations spend a lot of money before the assessment centre on selecting graduates (advertising, the milkround, interviews).

Any organisation that runs assessment centres will most probably have an intensive management training programme which itself is expensive. It's pointless putting people through that if they're not suitable in the first place.

Besides, it's unfair to the graduates they've selected. As this book has tried to show, objectivity works both ways – for the benefit of the organisation and of the candidate.

IT SOUNDS LIKE AN EXHAUSTING PROCESS

Assessment centres are hectic, concentrated hard work for
assessors. Their day starts with briefings long before you
arrive, goes on late into the night as they write up their notes,
and continues long after you've left. They have to stick to a
strict timetable to make sure that every candidate gets the
same amount of time and attention.

The timetable is also complex. Another way of building
objectivity into the process is to rotate assessors, with at least
one assessor being new to each candidate on each exercise, and
avoiding the same assessors working together.

By the final stage, ie after all the exercises and interviews are
finished, most of the assessors will have formed independent
views of each candidate.

WHAT DO ASSESSORS DO WHEN THEY'VE SEEN EVERYONE?

Assessment is a process of accumulating evidence from the
various tests and exercises for assembly at the final stage.
Throughout the assessment centre each assessor has been
classifying and evaluating evidence on the people that they've
observed. They then refine it on to a summary sheet under
profile criteria for each candidate.

For example, evidence of 'planning ability' can be gathered
from the project, the physical tasks (both group and 'own
command'), the individual obstacle test, the presentations, and
from information about past life obtained in the interviews.

After this, the assessors gather for the final evaluation
conference.

WHAT HAPPENS TO ALL THE INFORMATION THEY'VE GOT ABOUT ME?

At the final evaluation conference, all preliminary ratings - from all the exercises and from every assessor who has observed you – are brought together into a single matrix. Each rating for each criterion is kept separate.

The conference also is where other information about you from all sources (psychometric and numeracy tests, personal skills, outside reports and references, CV or application form) is pooled. From all this data, the conference members (who are the chair and the assessors) get a picture of you as you relate to the profile of criteria that was drawn up in the first place.

HOW DO THE ASSESSORS DISCUSS THE EVIDENCE?

It is at the evaluation conference that the significance of accurately recorded and classified evidence becomes apparent. Assessors have to justify their evaluations by refering to the data they have obtained. Moreover, some assessors may have to make judgements on the strength of reports of exercises they have not observed – hence the emphasis placed on accuracy, clarity and correct context.

Even if a candidate is clearly not going to be accepted, he or she will be discussed in as much depth as someone who is.

HOW LONG DOES THE CONFERENCE LAST?

It's a lengthy process of discussing evidence about each candidate that comes from different knowledge and different perspectives. For example, an interview with a technical line manager will give a different dimension from that of a candidate's behaviour during a group discussion.

The group does not look for absolutes but for trends with regard to strengths and weaknesses. No decision to select or reject is made before all aspects have been discussed.

WHAT ELSE DO THE ASSESSORS TAKE INTO ACCOUNT WHEN COMING TO THEIR DECISION?

They also consider the relative importance of the criteria. For example, one organisation may rate leadership skills more highly than another might. A firm of solicitors would probably need more of the critical thinking skills than numeracy.

At the beginning of this book we described the research and work that goes into designing an assessment centre, and we mentioned that the organisation's management training programme also influences the angle that the assessment takes.

WHY DO FUTURE MANAGEMENT TRAINING PROGRAMMES BECOME A FACTOR AT THIS STAGE?

The assessors also take into account the individual's potential and their need for development in specified areas, especially those in which the assessment centre exercises have indicated that the candidate is lacking. The assessors need to know the organisation's training programme well and they are able to judge whether a candidate would benefit from it.

When debating a weakness in a candidate (and there's no such thing as a perfect candidate – everyone has weaknesses!) they decide whether their programme is able to remedy it. As organisations' programmes vary in both content and length, it follows that they differ in their ability to develop certain skills.

ONE OF THE STUDENTS ON MY COURSE SEEMS TO BE GOOD AT EVERYTHING! I'M SURE SHE'LL PUT EVERYONE ELSE AT AN ASSESSMENT CENTRE IN THE SHADE!

Don't be too sure! All candidates are limited or inadequate in some areas. The assessors make allowances for age and previous experience. Anyway, candidates are never compared with one another - they're judged against a standard, namely the profile of the ideal person to work for that organisation. It's quite possible for everyone at an assessment centre to be rejected or for everyone to be accepted.

IT MUST BE EASY FOR THE ASSESSORS IF THEY GET AN OUTSTANDING PERSON COMING THROUGH THE ASSESSMENT CENTRE. BUT NO-ONE'S PERFECT, SO A LOT OF CANDIDATES MUST BE BORDERLINE

Yes – it's this marginal area that's the most difficult. That is when the assessors return to the raw data and the first observations they recorded. You can now see the importance of accurate and objective recording, and why they have to be so well trained in it.

The occupational psychologists are aware of the difficulties that arise in rating borderline candidates and will define the middle grades very finely within each criterion and behavioural indicator.

31

MY FRIEND WENT THROUGH COMPANY X's ASSESSMENT CENTRE LAST YEAR. SHE'LL BE ABLE TO GIVE ME ALL THE INSIDE INFORMATION

Fine – but don't rely on it! Things may have changed since then. Organisations modify the exercises they do on a regular basis, so you may encounter something quite unexpected, although the general principles remain the same.

The rate of change in the modern world is very rapid, especially due to the impact of technology, and successful organisations have to adapt. Future job requirements get redefined in response to changes within organisations, and it follows that the criteria are being regularly revised. The shelf life of assessment centre exercises is reducing and it is becoming necessary to redesign them every few years.

Also, organisations try to keep one step ahead of candidates. They know that graduates are getting more exposure to assessment centre techniques and that students are therefore becoming more sophisticated. They are also aware that there are 'leakage' problems through the campus grapevine, so don't expect the same exercises.

WILL I EVER KNOW THE DETAILS OF WHAT EMERGED ON MY PERFORMANCE AT AN ASSESSMENT CENTRE?

If you get accepted, some organisations use the information to feed back to candidates directly, highlighting their strengths and development needs, and subsequently construct a first set of performance objectives for the trainee. This information can form the basis of his or her personal development plan, continuing education and training. If you don't get accepted, most organisations are willing to tell you why.

IS THIS THE LAST TIME I'LL ENCOUNTER AN ASSESSMENT CENTRE?

By no means. More and more organisations are using them at different stages in their employees' careers to diagnose their further development needs. They may also use them for selecting internal candidates for promotion.

WHAT ELSE CAN I EXPECT AT THE END OF AN ASSESSMENT CENTRE?

Some organisations take the opportunity to research the effectiveness of their graduate recruitment brochure, the milkround, campus presentations, and their corporate image in general. They may even research your reaction to the assessment centre you've just been through.

Nowadays, organisations are very conscious of their public image and that includes their image on campus. They want you to have enjoyed your experience with them and for you to feel that you've benefited from it in some way. They do not want it to be an event that leaves you with a bad impression.

I'VE JUST HEARD THAT I'VE FAILED COMPANY X's ASSESSMENT CENTRE. I FEEL VERY DEPRESSED

It's not a question of pass or fail. Assessment centres do not consist of examinations where there's a right or a wrong answer. Human beings are not that cut and dried and their abilities tend to fall into a spectrum.

The exercises are designed to find out whether there's a 'fit' between you and the job the organisation is selecting for. An assessment centre can be described as shining a very narrow beam, from a certain angle, on particular aspects – your personality, abilities, character and intellect *but only* from the point of view of what the organisation wants. Other than technical knowledge, you're not being tested on what you know. If you are not accepted, it does *not* mean that you should feel rejected as a person. It's a bit like (although far more scientific!) falling in love – the 'chemistry' has to be right on both sides.

It works both ways – if the organisation does not accept you, it means that that organisation is wrong for you. Far better to find out now than to waste a miserable couple of years in a job you hate.

HOW CAN I BENEFIT FROM THIS EXPERIENCE?

Most organisations will give you feedback on how you did at the assessment centre, either by telephone or else in writing. This can be very valuable for you to plan your future career development and direction. You have to be quite strong however, to take criticism. It may hurt – but once you've got over that, be objective about yourself and decide how you can remedy your weaknesses. For instance, it's relatively easy to remedy any lack of computer skills.

Learning about yourself and taking responsibility for who you are both form part of the maturing process. It will stand you in good stead whether or not you've been accepted by Company X. And, of course, it's excellent experience for your next interview or assessment centre!

However, if you really hated the whole assessment centre process in itself, it may be better to make your approaches to organisations through application forms and interviews. Also, think of applying to smaller organisations that are less likely to use the system, and where you can shine as an individual.

WILL MY RESULTS BE PASSED ON TO ANY OTHER ORGANISATION?

No reputable recruiter would ever do so, especially if they're held on computer where they're covered by the Data Protection Act.

HOW CAN I PREPARE FOR AN ASSESSMENT CENTRE?

- The most important thing is to go in with the right frame of mind. For most people, it's an enjoyable experience during which they learn a lot about themselves.
- Most careers services hold assessment centre trials – take advantage of these.
- Get practice on the numerical and verbal reasoning tests and psychometric tests – again, enquire at your careers centre. Being familiar with them will make you feel a lot more confident.
- Scientists and engineers should pay particular attention to verbal reasoning tests as they are often more at ease with calculations, diagrams and formulae than words. Recruiters repeatedly remark on these candidates' lack of communication skills as well as their lack of commercial awareness.
- Most university courses nowadays contain projects and group work. These are excellent experience. The assessment centre exercises require you to demonstrate skills similar to those your work has developed – analysing and thinking things through, prioritising, reaching a decision, communicating the results both verbally (in the form of a presentation) and in writing.

DOS AND DON'TS OF ASSESSMENT CENTRES

DON'T:

- Set out to impress the assessors – just be yourself, concentrate on what you're being asked to do and think things through. They will soon find out if you're pretending to be someone other than who you are.
- Remember that the main purpose of assessment centres is to select people, not to reject, so go there with a positive frame of mind.
- Compete against the other candidates. You're being measured against a standard, not compared with anyone else. Don't ever try to put someone else down, score points or crush their confidence. You, and others in your group, will do best if you work in a spirit of co-operation so that *your* positive abilities can be shown to the best advantage.
- Try to dominate your group. Leaders lead through respect, not bullying. It's your common sense, your intellect and the quality of your decisions that will get intelligent people to follow you. Negotiate rather than confront.

DO:

- Practise basic skills like numeracy – without a calculator. Learn to estimate quickly but in the written tests, don't sacrifice accuracy for speed.
- Be aware of the time factor. Because all work nowadays is so driven, and because assessment centre exercises and tests

are all timed and concentrated, you need to be have a sense of urgency. However, don't panic – detach yourself and calmly think the problem through before rushing into a decision.

- Concentrate on the exercises, not on the impression you're making on the assessors or other candidates. Think hard about the problems, visualise the circumstances, think of alternative solutions.
- Show sensitivity to other people – if you're confronted with a problem to do with a person, try to find out why they're behaving in such a way. Your reaction to others is a vital part of team working and it's one of the things assessors will be looking for.
- Listen carefully to the contributions of others in your group and develop them if you think they're constructive. Don't just push your point of view.
- At the interview, be prepared to expand on any of the facts you have written down in the application form about yourself and your achievements, abilities and experiences.
- Although the selection procedure is blind to irrelevancies like background or manner, do dress neatly and appropriately. If you're going to do physical tasks, you'll be given or advised to bring suitable clothing, so you won't have to mess up that smart suit you've just bought especially for your job search.
- RELAX (easier said than done!) – and show what a friendly, dynamic, lively, motivated person you are. Stay calm and think things through before you react. On the other hand, it's not a good idea to come over as a shrinking violet, so try to strike a balance.

Remember – assessors want you to do your best and they would rather select than reject.